Nell Gets a Hat

By Carmel Reilly

Nell and Mum set off
for The Dell.

They will get a sun hat
for Nell.

The Dell has the best shops.

The shops sell many hats.

"Do you like this hat with a shell, Nell?" said Mum.

"Well, I like it," said Nell.
"But I want a pink hat."

Nell picked a pink hat
off the bench.

"I can tell that hat will be
too big," said Mum.

"This shop must sell a pink hat that fits me," said Nell.

Then, a red thing fell off the bench.

Nell picked it up.

"Look!" she said.

Nell put the red cap on.

It had a long flap.

She let out a yell.

"This cap is the one!"

CHECKING FOR MEANING

1. Where do Mum and Nell go shopping? *(Literal)*

2. Which hat does Mum show Nell first? *(Literal)*

3. Why might Nell need a hat? *(Inferential)*

EXTENDING VOCABULARY

Dell	What does the word *dell* mean? What is another word with a similar meaning? Why might the shopping area have been called *The Dell*?
shops	Look at the word *shops*. What sound does it start with? How many letters make this sound? What other words do you know that start with *sh*?
flap	What part of the hat in the story is the *flap*? Why does the hat have a flap? What other things have flaps?

MOVING BEYOND THE TEXT

1. What are some different sorts of hats?

2. Why do people wear hats?

3. What other clothing do people wear to help keep them safe from the sun?

4. If you could choose any hat, what would it look like? Why?

SPEED SOUNDS

at	an	ap	et	og	ug

ell	ack	ash	ing

PRACTICE WORDS

Dell

Nell

sell

Well

shell

tell

fell

yell